THE JEWISH HOLIDAY HOME COMPANION

A Parent's Guide to Family Celebration

Written by
Nicolas D. Mandelkern
Vicki L. Weber

In consultation with
Rabbi Hyman Chanover
Rabbi Morrison David Bial

D0684046

BEHRMAN HOUSE

PROJECT EDITOR: RUBY G. STRAUSS

BOOK DESIGN: BARBARA HUNTLEY

COVER DESIGN: ROBERT J. O'DELL

The editor and publisher gratefully acknowledge the cooperation of the following sources of photographs for this book:

FPG International/Ron Chapple, 9; Francene Keery Cover (top and bottom left), 12, 14 19, 23, 30, 32, 40, 46, 58, 66, 68; The Jewish Community Center of Cleveland 21; Bill Aron Cover (top and bottom right), 26, 50; From the Collection of the Hebrew Union College Skirball Museum 29, 57; The Jewish Museum 31, 41, 48; Israeli Consulate 35; The New York Public Library 38; The United Nations 53.

INTRODUCTION:
HOW TO USE THIS HANDBOOK

This Holiday Home Companion is designed to help you bring the holidays alive in your own home. Shared holiday experiences will draw you and your child together in a unique closeness. Judaism is primarily a home-focused way of life. Each holiday, with its home symbols, rituals, food, music, and tales, brings delight to the family and, in turn, beauty and joy to living as a Jew.

The first section of the handbook, an *Introduction to the Holidays* (pages 8-68), contains a short chapter on each holiday that provides a little of its history and the ways it is celebrated at home and in the synagogue. Suggestions for actively involving your children in the celebration of each holiday are also included.

The second section, *Home Rituals for the Holidays* (pages 69-87), is a reference to help you choose rituals to perform as you begin celebrating a holiday at home, or to add to home celebrations you already enjoy. The section contains the blessings, prayers, and songs usually included in the home service for each holiday. The text of the blessings and prayers is provided in both English and Hebrew along with a transliteration. A calendar listing the secular dates of the Jewish holidays is included to aid you in your planning (page 88).

Finally, because the flavor of so many holidays comes from the special foods we eat, some popular holiday recipes are provided in the third section (pages 89-96).

You don't have to know everything about the Jewish festivals. Your child cares less about how much you *know* and more about how you *feel*. When you require answers to your child's questions, turn to this handbook for guidance. Beyond that, you can always ask the rabbi or a Jewish educator.

If you have not been celebrating the holidays at home, we hope this handbook will encourage you to begin. If you have already established some home rituals for the holidays, we hope you will find some ideas here to increase your enjoyment of these special times and to help you build a cycle of home celebrations that truly belongs to you and your family.

CONTENTS

II HOME RITUALS FOR THE HOLIDAYS

III HOLIDAY RECIPES

INTRODUCTION
TO THE
HOLIDAYS

DAYS OF AWE

Wholeness and holiness we seek as we enter a new year.
The Rabbinical Assembly Mahzor

For centuries, the High Holy Days have captivated the Jewish people with a mysterious and inescapable bond. The call of the shofar on Rosh Hashanah rouses us from summer drowsiness, giving us a fresh supply of spiritual energy at a time when we seem to need it most. For the next ten days we feel ourselves drawing closer to God, until we reach the spiritual heights of Yom Kippur. It is a time of reflection: a time to reflect on the past, to marvel at the wonders of God's world, and to think about what we want ourselves and our children to become.

A thorough housecleaning is traditional and, because we want to be seen in our best light during this "time of judgment," new clothes help set these days apart as a special time.

In the weeks before Rosh Hashanah many people visit the graves of loved ones. This custom helps us consider our past as we prepare for a new year.

A medieval poet wrote, "On Rosh Hashanah it is written, and on Yom Kippur it is sealed." These words, which we recite during the Rosh Hashanah morning service, tie the two holidays together with a powerful image. Tradition says that on Rosh Hashanah, God writes judgments in the Book of Life, but the book remains open until Yom Kippur. During these ten days of repentance, we have the opportunity through prayer, the performance of *mitzvot* (righteous acts), and the resolve to become better people, to influence God's judgment—that is, to be "Sealed in the Book of Life." We can then let go of the old year, and the mistakes we made. Taking our children by the hand, we step together into the New Year.

ROSH HASHANAH

Renew us for a year that is good and sweet.
Rosh Hashanah Liturgy

The Hebrew words *Rosh Hashanah* mean "head of the year," and this day, the first of the Hebrew month Tishre, marks the beginning of the Jewish year. It also celebrates the creation of the world, for Jewish tradition tells us that God completed the seven days of Creation on Rosh Hashanah. Rosh Hashanah has several other names and meanings as well. From the Torah, it is *Yom Teruah*, the Day of Sounding the Shofar, a reminder of the covenant between God and the Jewish people. It is *Yom Hazikaron*, a "Day of Remembering," a time to review the past year, considering both the good we have done and the times when we did not measure up. It is also *Yom Hadin*, the "Day of Judgment." The Jewish tradition holds that we are evenly balanced: part good, part sinful. Thus one right-eous act, one *mitzvah*, can tip the scales in our favor, and we can be inscribed in the Book of Life.

AT HOME
Rosh Hashanah, like all Jewish holidays, begins in the evening. The Book of Nehemiah tells us how to celebrate the first night: "Eat rich food and drink sweet wine, and

share with those who have none" (8:10). Before the meal, the home festival service includes reciting the blessing over the candles, the Sheheḥeyanu (a blessing for special occasions), the Festival Kiddush over wine, and the blessing over bread, Ha-Motzi (see pages 72, 76, 77).

CUSTOMS AND TRADITIONS

The ḥallah for Rosh Hashanah is round rather than the traditional oval braided bread, and represents our cyclical sense of time. As one year ends and another begins, we come full circle like a wheel. Some sources liken the round ḥallah to a majestic crown, a symbol of God's sovereignty. We eat the ḥallah with apple slices dipped in honey to express our hope for a sweet year.

Generations of Jews have greeted each other with the traditional Rosh Hashanah refrain: "May you be inscribed for a good year!" In the last century, as families spread out over larger distances, people began sending these greetings through the mail on Rosh Hashanah cards. *"Shanah Tovah* - A Good Year!"

IN THE SYNAGOGUE

The focus of Rosh Hashanah is the synagogue rather than the home. This time of remembrance and judgment affects us not just as individuals, but as a community.

The themes of creation, remembrance, and redemption are echoed throughout the Rosh Hashanah liturgy. In our prayers we acknowledge God's sovereignty and we recognize our human failings.

The most striking aspect of the Rosh Hashanah services is the sounding of the shofar. This is the biblical injunction for the celebration of Rosh Hashanah: "In the seventh month, on the first day of the month, you shall observe a sacred occasion. You shall not work at your occupations. You shall observe it as a day when the shofar is sounded" (Numbers 29:1).

The shofar has inspired many interpretations. The Rabbis of Talmudic times heard the shofar as a sign of God's mercy. Maimonides, the great Jewish philosopher, heard it as a call to repentance.

When blown, the shofar produces a loud piercing sound.

The Bible cites the shofar in a variety of contexts. It was blown to announce the New Moon and to sound an alarm in times of crisis. For the prophet Isaiah, it hailed the coming of the messianic age: "And in that day a great shofar will sound." It is a thrilling fanfare, calling to mind ancient times, and reminding us of our covenant with God at Sinai.

The sounding of the shofar follows a very specific pattern that incorporates four distinct sounds. In Hebrew, these are:

tekiah, one long blast;

teruah, nine staccato blasts;

shevarim, three short blasts;

tekiah gedolah, one very long blast.

TASHLICH

In the afternoon, after Rosh Hashanah services, many people go to a nearby river or other body of flowing water. We empty our pockets of any crumbs and throw them into the waters, symbolic of ridding ourselves of our sins. "You will cast your sins into the depths of the sea" (Micah 7:19). The *Tashlich* ceremony, a refreshing outdoor contrast to the morning hours spent in the synagogue, helps us make a fresh start for the New Year.

Dipping apples in honey is a favorite Rosh Hashanah custom.

ROSH HASHANAH FOR CHILDREN

Although young children are not able to sit through long services, there are many ways to share the message of the holiday with children of all ages. Most synagogues now incorporate children's services into their Rosh Hashanah schedule. Of course, all children can participate in the home service. Making New Year's cards to send to friends and relatives is a particularly nice family project, and those with a flair for kitchen activities can try baking honey cake or making *taiglach*, a traditional honey candy (see recipe page 90).

YOM KIPPUR

Forgive and pardon our sins on this Day of Atonement.
Yom Kippur Confessional

More than anything else, Yom Kippur is about forgiveness. On Rosh Hashanah we began to review our shortcomings and successes of the past year. The days that follow provide the opportunity to apologize for our errors and seek forgiveness from those we may have wronged. This is *teshuvah*, or repentance. It is only after we have worked out our grievances among ourselves, forgiving and being forgiven by our families and friends, that we can then ask God's forgiveness. Yom Kippur is about our repentance, and God's mercy.

AT HOME

Yom Kippur is a solemn day, a day for thought and for prayer. Our focus is on the spiritual rather than the temporal, and to emphasize this, we fast from sundown to sundown. Fasting teaches us compassion. In our temporary deprivation, we remember that there are still people for whom hunger is present far more often than once a year. Fasting also points out our own human frailty and dependence upon God. A simple fact, but how easily we forget it: without food, we cannot live. Tradition requires adults to fast, but not young children, the elderly, nor the sick.

The eve of Yom Kippur is ushered in with a hearty meal. After the table is cleared, and before we set off for evening services, we light a *yahrzeit* candle in remembrance of family members who are no longer alive. This memorial candle burns throughout Yom Kippur. Yom Kippur candles are lit and the blessing is recited (see page 73). Some families spread a clean tablecloth and set out books in place of plates, to show that Yom Kippur is a day for study and contemplation rather than feasting and festivities. Finally, it is customary for parents to bless their children (see page 74).

IN THE SYNAGOGUE

The evening service takes its name from the famous prayer *Kol Nidre*, noted for its sad yet beautiful melody. Written in Aramaic, it is traditionally sung by the cantor. In *Kol Nidre*, we ask for God's understanding and forgiveness for the vows we made to God that we are unable to keep. A vow is a holy promise and we ask for forgiveness.

On the following day, the service is very long. In the *Al Ḥet* prayer, we confess our sins as a congregation, accepting responsibility not only for our own misdeeds, but for those of our family and community as well. Also included a number of times during Yom Kippur services is the *Avinu Malkenu* ("Our Parent, our Ruler,") a prayer asking God to forgive us despite our failings.

Yom Kippur services include *Yizkor*, the memorial service for the dead, and two Torah readings. During the afternoon service we read the Book of Jonah, with its story of the people of an evil city who repent their ways and are forgiven by God.

The concluding service of Yom Kippur is *Ne'ilah*, from *Ne'ilat ha-Sh'arim* or the closing of the gates. Some rabbis thought this referred to the closing of the Temple gates; others have said it refers to the gates of heaven, closing as the Book of Life is sealed. *Ne'ilah* ends with one last blast of the shofar and the cry, "Next year in Jerusalem!"

BREAKING THE FAST

At the close of the *Ne'ilah* Service, some synagogues invite their congregants to break the fast together with a light snack. Later, at home, we enjoy a special meal shared with family and friends, perhaps inviting people who would otherwise be alone. It is a joyful evening after a long and solemn day. We feel reinvigorated for the year that lies ahead.

TZEDAKAH

The message of Yom Kippur goes beyond repentance and forgiveness. As we look back on the mistakes of the past year, we think about how to improve ourselves. But, as Jews, we also ask ourselves how we can improve the world. This is the spirit of tzedakah, the way we help others. In the synagogue it may mean special fund-raising drives to support the United Jewish Appeal or other charitable organizations. At home it can mean any special effort or project to aid people less fortunate than ourselves.

YOM KIPPUR FOR CHILDREN

Even young children can be guided to an understanding of the message of repentance, forgiveness and change for the better, which are the hallmarks of Yom Kippur. Many synagogues offer special children's or family services. Obviously, fasting is not for young children, but they might want to make a partial attempt, skipping a meal or not eating candy or snacks.

Consider a family tzedakah project. Your children can save money to give to the poor. Together, you can visit someone who is ill, or volunteer in a soup kitchen. Activities like these help to teach children that when we become better people, we can help to make the world a better place.

SUKKOT

In order that future generations may know that I made the Israelites live in sukkot when I brought them out of Egypt.
Leviticus 23:42,43

The Bible calls Sukkot "*The* Festival." Already ancient by the time of King Solomon, it was one of the most important holidays of the year. In the fall, with the harvest safely stored, the Israelites commenced a week-long celebration of thanksgiving. Many went on pilgrimage to Jerusalem. There they stayed in makeshift little huts which eventually lent their name, *sukkot*, to the festival itself.

Later generations saw a symbolic connection between those huts and the tents of the Israelites in the Sinai wilderness. For them the holiday became a reminder of our ultimate dependence on God. Today we build big sturdy houses and buy our food in supermarkets, but once a year, we sit in a fragile little sukkah, open to wind and sky, and remember our own limitations.

Many commentators linked the sukkot to the huts built by our ancestors at harvest time. These farmers had to work continuously, lest the produce rot in the fields, so they built little huts close to their fields and worked from first light to darkness.

Today we sit in the sukkah at our leisure. In the pleasant evening air, we sing and eat in the sukkah, lingering as long as the weather permits. Some people even sleep overnight in their sukkah.

AT HOME

The Rabbis gave detailed instructions to sukkah builders. A sukkah must have at least three walls. These can be made of the flimsiest of materials, even cloth as long as it does not tear in strong wind. The roof is covered with leaves or branches, thick enough to give shade but sparse enough to let you see the stars at night. The structure is decorated with fruits, vegetables, artwork,

The sukkah is a perfect instrument for delighting and instructing children. Those who bemoan the absence of a Christmas tree in Jewish tradition have probably never given the sukkah a thought.

or anything festive and special. The construction is done before the holiday; some families begin to build a sukkah right after breaking the fast on Yom Kippur.

A mystical tradition holds that certain of our ancestors come to sit with us in the sukkah. They are called *ushpizin*-- "holy guests." When we enter the sukkah, we stand in the doorway and greet them with an ancient welcome: "I invite to my meal, honored spiritual guests Abraham, Isaac, Jacob, Joseph, Moses, Aaron, and David." In recent times, some have expanded the list of *ushpizin* to include important women of the Bible: Sarah, Rachel, Rebecca, Leah, Miriam, Abigail, and Esther.

The *Zohar*, a collection of mystical lore, warns that the *ushpizin* will not join our celebration unless we also invite the poor. This teaching reminds us of the Jewish tradition of hospitality. Honor the *ushpizin* by inviting family, friends, and neighbors to your sukkah.

The holiday opens in the sukkah with the candle blessing, Kiddush, and Ha-Motzi (see pages 72, 76, 77). The Sheheheyanu blessing is added on the first night of the festival. Then comes a special blessing for Sukkot followed by a festival meal. Interestingly, there are no particular foods associated directly with Sukkot.

IN THE SYNAGOGUE
On Sukkot, the priests of the Second Temple performed an elaborately choreographed ritual. Our own

festival observance preserves some of those ancient ceremonies.

For example, many Jews come to Sukkot morning services carrying a lulav and etrog, known collectively as the "four species." The etrog is a lemon-like fruit or citron. The lulav bundle contains three different types of tree twigs: palm, myrtle, and willow. Their use as ceremonial objects goes back to biblical times: "On the first day, you shall take the fruit of a goodly tree (etrog), palm branches, thick boughs of trees (myrtle), and willows and rejoice before God" (Leviticus 23:40). Some rabbis have likened each of the four species to different types of Jews; while held together they symbolize the unity of the Jewish people.

A special blessing is recited over the lulav and etrog (see page 80).

During the synagogue service the lulav is shaken in every direction—to the front, to the right, to the back, to the left, up and down—demonstrating our recognition that God is everywhere.

THE EIGHTH DAY OF SUKKOT

Sukkot closes with the holiday of Shemini Atzeret, an "Assembly of the Eighth Day." Originally Shemini Atzeret was a day of meditation and rest. Like other holidays, Shemini Atzeret took on a second day in the Diaspora. By the eleventh century, that second day became a separate holiday—the irrepressible Simḥat Torah. In Liberal congregations Shemini Atzeret and Simḥat Torah are celebrated on the same day.

SUKKOT FOR CHILDREN

The sukkah is a perfect instrument for delighting and instructing children. Building and decorating a sukkah can be a family project in which children of all ages can participate. Paper chains, drawings, paintings, and photographs, in addition to fruits and flowers, make colorful, lively additions to the sukkah. Some families save their Rosh Hashanah cards to hang in the sukkah as well. The length of the holiday also provides many opportunities for children to invite their own guests to join family meals in the sukkah.

SIMHAT TORAH

Turn it (the Torah) again and again, for everthing is in it.
Avot 2:8

Simhat Torah, translated as "rejoicing in the Torah," celebrates the annual cycle of Torah reading. On Simhat Torah we finish the last portion of Deuteronomy and begin, again, with the first chapter of Genesis. The holiday could have evolved into a dry salute to scholarship, but it is instead a dancing and singing holiday, one that has been compared to a joyous wedding. It brings the Torah closer to all of us, scholar and nonscholar, adult and child.

IN THE SYNAGOGUE

Adults are called up to the Torah to chant the blessings, an *aliyah*. In some synagogues, the last *aliyah* is given to all the children. A large *tallit*, prayer shawl, is held over their heads and everyone in the congregation chants the Torah blessings with them.

During the service, every Torah scroll is taken out of the Ark, or *Aron Hakodesh*. Singing songs, we parade around the synagogue in a series of seven processions called *hakkafot*—circlings. By the end of the last *hakkafah*, everyone who wants to has carried the Torah. Children wave flags and march along too. Some scholars have likened these flags to the twelve tribal banners of ancient Israel.

SIMHAT TORAH FOR CHILDREN

With its dancing, flag waving, and wonderful sense of abandon, Simhat Torah is a holiday with particular appeal for children. They can make their own flags to wave and cap the celebration with jelly apples and other sweets.

In the synagogue on Simhat Torah every Torah is taken from the Ark and carried in a series of processions called *hakkafot*.

[26]

ḤANUKKAH

And so they kept the dedication of the altar eight days.
I Maccabees 4:59

During the darkest season of the year, Ḥanukkah comes into our lives with a cheerful combination of games and gifts, songs and stories, light and laughter. It occurs near the winter solstice, when days are short but promise to lengthen once again. A hint of that promise comes from the Ḥanukkah candles, glowing warmly against the bleak background of deep winter.

Although Ḥanukkah is the only major holiday that has no basis in the Bible, it is the best documented of all the Jewish holidays. Its story is so simple yet so powerful that it cannot fail to captivate even a young child. In 168 B.C.E. a small group of Jews, led by Judah "The Maccabee," rebelled against the Greek culture forced on them by the Syrian rulers. They refused to submit to the new order of Antiochus IV, King of Syria, who had outlawed many Jewish practices and placed idols in the Temple in Jerusalem. The Maccabees fought a bold campaign of guerrilla warfare, attacking and retreating to camps hidden in the Judean hills. Despite tremendous odds, they drove the Syrian-Greeks out of the land.

In the month of Kislev in the year 165 B.C.E., the Maccabees rededicated the Temple to Jewish worship. They then celebrated with an eight-day festival. The holiday's name, Ḥanukkah, comes from the Hebrew word for "dedication."

Five hundred years later, the Rabbis of the Talmud reexamined the message of Ḥanukkah. Instead of emphasizing a military battle to keep Judaism alive, they spoke of God's miraculous way. When the Maccabees purified the Temple, the Talmud tells us, they found a small vial of oil for the Temple lamp, containing enough to last only one day. Eight days later, the menorah still burned! In recounting this miracle, the Rabbis lifted Ḥanukkah from its historical context. More than a commemoration of victory in war, Ḥanukkah now celebrated faith in God.

AT HOME

The menorah stands as the most compelling symbol of Ḥanukkah. In ancient times it stood in the Temple in Jerusalem, a symbol of Jewish peoplehood long before the Maccabees' revolt. The original seven-branched menorah is first mentioned in the Bible, but on Ḥanukkah we use one with nine branches, called a *hanukkiah*. Eight lights represent the eight days of the holiday, and the ninth, called the *shamash*, is used to light the others (see page 81).

A special song for Ḥanukkah is *Maoz Tzur* ("Rock of Ages"). For twenty-five generations or more, Jews have sung these words at Ḥanukkah after the lighting of the candles. When you sing *Maoz Tzur*, your voices join with theirs (see page 83).

A hanukkiah comes in many shapes and sizes.
This one, crafted in silver, burns oil.

Hannukah Lamp 27.70 Germany 1814, dedication by Samuel Hirsch, silver, repousse, cast pierced, engraved. From the collection of Hebrew Union College Skirball Museum, Erich Hockley Photographer.

Some people serve latkes with apple sauce; others prefer sour cream (see recipe on page 92).

Celebrating the miracle of the oil extends to food as well. Few of us can resist the delicious aroma and hearty flavor of latkes, the potato pancakes that are the holiday's enduring dish. It is also traditional during these festival days to indulge in doughnuts and other fried foods.

ḤANUKKAH FOR CHILDREN

After the candles and the latkes, it's time for the special Ḥanukkah game—the dreidel game. Candy, nuts, raisins, or Ḥanukkah *gelt* (money) supply the "pot" in this traditional game from Eastern Europe.

To play, everyone puts some of their *gelt* into the pot. Each player spins the dreidel in turn. The letters on the dreidel represent four different instructions in Yiddish:

נ , nun, for *nisht* (nothing). Player receives nothing.

ג , gimmel, for *ganz* (all). Player gets the whole pot.

ה, hay, for *halb* (half). Player gets half.

שׁ, shin, for *shtell* (put). Player contributes *gelt* to the pot.

There is also a Hebrew saying associated with the four letters. They stand for:

Nes Gadol Hayah Sham.

"A Great Miracle Happened There."

In Israel, the Hebrew letter *pay* (for the word *po)* appears on the dreidel: "A Great Miracle Happened **Here!**"

[31]

The practice of giving children small amounts of money, or *gelt*, for Ḥanukkah is an old Eastern European custom. It probably had its origins in the tzedakah, or charity, given to needy students at Ḥanukkah time so they could finish their Torah studies. In the United States, Jews have expanded the custom of *gelt*-giving to a more elaborate exchange of gifts, adding a new layer of joy to an already happy holiday. Children might also choose a toy to donate to charity, thus emphasizing the special tradition of tzedakah in Judaism.

TU B'SHEVAT

As the days of a tree, so shall be the days of My People.
Isaiah 65:22

Winter is almost over and we eagerly await the first signs of spring. Daylight hours begin to lengthen and before very long the stark gray of the tree branches will be softened with misty green as new buds swell and new shoots seek out the warmth of the sun. It is time to celebrate Tu B'Shevat—the new year for trees.

The practical need for a "birthday" for trees arises from a Torah commandment:

> *And when you come to the land and have*
> *planted all manner of trees for food, the fruit*
> *thereof shall be forbidden for three years; you shall*
> *not eat it. In the fourth year, all the fruit thereof*
> *shall be holy and must be given to God. But in the*
> *fifth year, you may eat the fruit, that it may yield*
> *unto you more richly the increase thereof.*
> *(Leviticus 19:23-25)*

In Talmudic times, the Rabbis chose the fifteenth day of the month of Shevat to mark the yearly aging of all trees. After the destruction of the Second Temple and the

[33]

exile of Jews from their land, Tu B'Shevat also became a special link to Israel—a day to eat fruits associated with Eretz Yisrael. Later, as Jews began to return to settle in Israel during the late 1800's, they planted trees in order to revive the barren land, and Tu B'Shevat became a holiday for Jews all over the world to contribute to the greening of Israel.

AT HOME

Many Jews celebrate Tu B'Shevat with a special seder that features many Israeli fruits and four different kinds of wine.

The fruits fall into three groups: those without pits, shells, or inedible peel, such as figs, raisins, grapes, and berries; those with pits but no shells or peel, such as olives, plums, and dates; and those lacking pits but with outer layers that must be removed, such as oranges, grapefruits, almonds, and pomegranates.

Although the order of the ritual often varies, the seder itself consists of "courses" of each type of fruit, each course followed by a cup of wine. The first cup of wine is red, the second is red with a few drops of white, the third is white with a little red, and the fourth cup is white wine.

TREE PLANTING

In Israel, Tu B'Shevat is a national holiday celebrated with tree-planting ceremonies. For over ninety years, the

Jewish National Fund has planted trees in Israel with contributions from Jews around the world. Through the J.N.F. we can plant trees to commemorate many special events or special people. A tradition has developed to plant trees in honor of a new baby, in honor of a relative or friend who becomes Bar or Bat Mitzvah, or in memory of someone who dies.

The Jewish National Fund has planted over 200 million trees in Israel.

TU B'SHEVAT FOR CHILDREN

Making a family contribution to the Jewish National Fund or planting a tree in one's own yard are special and natural ways to celebrate Tu B'Shevat. Young children, however, may also enjoy a project with more immediacy. Simple indoor gardens can capture their imagination as they watch new green shoots breaking through the black earth. Bean sprouts or alfalfa are good choices because they sprout quickly. Or, you may wish to grow your own parsley to use for the coming Passover seder. Some synagogues have a formal tree planting on their grounds as part of the festivities of the holiday.

Tu B'Shevat is also a time to consider our more general connection to the earth and our obligation to take care of it. The Jewish tradition of *tikkun olam*—repairing the world—can be taken in an ecological as well as a spiritual sense. On this day, then, we can renew our commitment to this philosophy by planning a family recycling project.

PURIM

Make them days of feasting and gladness, and of sending portions
one to another, and gifts to the poor.
Megillat Esther 9:22

We make noise in the synagogue, we parade in costumes, and we let the kids stay up late. It's Purim and it's time to bend the rules.

The Purim story, though full of melodrama, plot twists, and palace intrigue, stresses themes of Jewish unity and courage in the face of anti-Semitism. Esther, the young Jewish queen of Persian King Ahasuerus, risked her life to convince the monarch not to allow his evil advisor Haman to kill the Jews.

An ambitious man, Haman tried to use fear of the Jews to consolidate his own power. He cited the classic argument of anti-Semites: "They follow different laws and customs from everyone else." He appealed to human greed, urging Persians to kill the Jews and take their possessions.

The Purim story also demonstrates the importance of courage. King Ahasuerus did not hate the Jews, nor did most of his subjects. But neither did they care enough to save them. When Haman presented his terrible plan to kill the Jews, King Ahasuerus unthinkingly agreed.

Haman, by a throw of the dice called "lots" (*purim*), chose the thirteenth of Adar as the day to eliminate the Jews. Only the efforts of Esther and her cousin Mordecai defeated Haman. Only the vigilance of these heroes thwarted the enemy and rescued the Jews of Persia. As a result, Haman was unable to murder the Jews and was himself hanged for his evil plot.

Engraving of Queen Esther—Gustave Dore.

According to the Book of Esther, the Jews of Persia took up arms against their enemies. But today we celebrate Purim with humor, a most nonviolent weapon.

[38]

We defeat our enemy Haman by laughing at him, drowning out his name in a sea of noise.

AT HOME

The fanciful celebrations of Purim call for costumes and masks, Purim gifts and hamantashen.

The practice of dressing in costume on Purim began in Italy during the fifteenth century. Italian Jews were probably imitating the Mardi Gras Carnival, which occurs around the same time of year as Purim. In borrowing from another culture, Italian Jews were actually reclaiming an ancient tradition. Carnival and Purim may share the same ancestor, a festival of early spring celebrated by Jews along with other peoples of the ancient Near East. Later the Book of Esther gave the festival its distinctly Jewish flavor and moral overtones.

Let your creativity flow when you design costumes. You can turn your children and yourselves into kings and queens, cowboys and clowns. A costume alters our identity, shielding us from the world and its restrictive demands. From behind a mask we play with reality, adopting and dropping roles as we please.

Purim's most recognizable and edible symbol is hamantashen, triangular cookies enclosing poppy seed or fruit filling. Their shape reminds us of Haman's three-cornered hat. In Israel the confection is called *oznai Haman*, Haman's ears.

TZEDAKAH

The Book of Esther records a letter sent by Mordecai to Jews throughout the Persian Empire. He proclaimed the fourteenth and fifteenth days of the month of Adar to be "days of feasting and joy, days for sending presents to one another and gifts to the poor." Today on Purim, as on many other holidays, we undertake charitable acts of tzedakah.

Also on Purim, we put together special baskets of fruit, cookies, or other food, called *Mishloaḥ Manot*, and send or take them to friends and relatives. In this way we fulfill Mordecai's edict and rejoice in the happiness of the day.

In Israel, hamantashen are called *oznai Haman*, Haman's ears, as he was thought to have triangular shaped ones (see recipe on page 93).

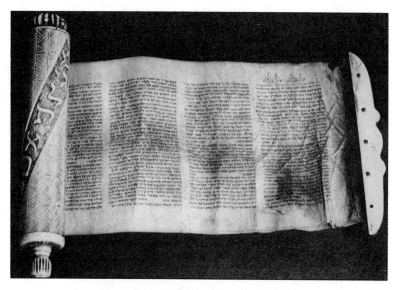

Scroll of Esther with carved ivory case.

IN THE SYNAGOGUE

The Hebrew word *megillah* means a hand-written scroll. It can refer to five different texts, but when we say *The* Megillah, we are talking about only one: the Book of Esther, our source for the events of the Purim story. It is read publicly in the synagogue during the Purim evening and morning services.

We don't know if the events in the Book of Esther really happened. (In fact, unlike Ḥanukkah, there is no historical evidence in support of the Purim story, and some of its details conflict with historians' knowledge of Persia.) Nevertheless, we enjoy the Megillah simply for its exciting story. Thanks to a skillful, anonymous writer, the book reads almost like a modern suspense novel.

Everyone participates in the Megillah reading. At every mention of Haman's name, we make as much noise as we can. We use *graggers* (the Yiddish name for noise-makers); we stamp our feet; we yell, hiss, and boo. We defeat Haman by laughing at him and drowning out the sound of his evil name.

PURIM FOR CHILDREN

The silliness, the noisiness, the dressing up: Purim is a natural for children. Homemade *graggers* are a favorite Purim craft. Your children will certainly want to help plan their Purim costumes. Also they can create their own picture Megillah to take to synagogue.

Children are natural actors for your own *Purimshpiel* as well. *Shpiel* is the Yiddish word for "play". First introduced by German Jews in the late Middle Ages, a *Purimshpiel* retells the Purim story on stage. The actors often used humor to disguise sharp criticism of the community or government. You and your children can create your own *Purimshpiel*. You need not confine yourself to the story of Mordecai and Esther; touch on anything else you think funny or important. A successful *Purimshpiel* will entertain the whole family.

PASSOVER

All people, in every generation, must regard themselves as having been personally freed from Egypt.

Haggadah

Children love to ask the question *why*. Our Rabbis knew that and built the observance of Passover around that very question. They also gave an answer, one that in two thousand years has not lost its power. When children ask the question, "How is this night different from all other nights?" they are answered with a retelling of the story of how we were freed from slavery in Egypt.

We retell the Passover story in the warm, inviting atmosphere of a family feast—the seder. The Rabbis designed the seder as a way of passing Jewish identity and awareness from parents to their children, from generation to generation. In fact, the name of the book containing the seder service, Haggadah, means "telling." It comes from the biblical phrase, "And you shall tell your child."

Passover celebrates beginnings. We look out the window and see new green shoots budding on the trees. Spring is here once again. The green vegetable or parsley on the seder plate symbolizes this seasonal rebirth.

Passover celebrates another beginning, our beginning as a free and independent people. The Book of Exodus captures those distant yet familiar events: Moses' confrontations with Pharaoh; the Ten Plagues; the hurried departure of the Hebrew slaves; the miraculous parting of the Sea of Reeds (the Red Sea). We are entranced by the drama and emotional content of the story, but we find it more difficult to understand that *we* were those Hebrews enslaved in Egypt. At the Passover seder we put ourselves inside that story. We perform ritual acts, dipping greens in salt water or spilling drops of wine.

AT HOME

Early in the seder, the Haggadah issues its famous invitation: "Let all who are hungry come and eat." Although we remember these words throughout the year, we heed them with special attention at Passover. Before the start of the holiday, it is traditional to give tzedakah. This gift of charity is called *maot hittim*, "money for wheat," because it enables poor families to buy matzah and other foods for the holidays.

Generations of Jews have greeted Passover with strenuous housecleaning to remove all traces of *hametz* or leaven—the substance that makes dough rise. Jewish tradition provides the reason for this spring cleaning. When the Hebrew slaves heard that Pharaoh would permit them to leave Egypt, they packed hurriedly, lest he change his mind. Carrying dough for bread on their backs, they let it bake in the desert sun. Later, God commanded the people to remember their deliverance from Egypt each year by eating matzah and avoiding all ḥametz.

A tradition evolved that adds drama to the prohibition of ḥametz. On the night before the seder, the family dims the lights and conducts a "search for leaven," *Bedikat Ḥametz*. Armed with a candle, a feather, a paper bag, and a wooden spoon, the family searches the house for those last remaining crumbs of bread. Because by this late hour most people have already finished their Passover cleaning, it became traditional to hide several pieces of ḥametz around the house prior to the search. Remember where you hide them, because you have to find every piece! In the morning, the ḥametz is burned outside the house. (For instructions, see page 84.)

THE SEDER

For centuries Jews commemorated the Exodus from Egypt with a pilgrimage to the Temple in Jerusalem. When the Temple was destroyed, our Rabbis developed new ways to keep the memory of the Exodus alive. One of these ways was the Seder, a ritual meal modeled after the elaborate banquets of the Greeks. Later generations added other readings and songs and set the order down in a book called the Haggadah.

[45]

The songs we sing at the seder were composed with children in mind. Many find the repetitious *Chad Gadya* and *Echad Mi Yodea* fun to sing.

Complete instructions for making a seder can be found in the Haggadah; highlights are presented here to get you started.

The centerpiece of the seder table is the seder plate containing the five ritual foods of Passover:

Zeroah, the roasted lamb bone, reminds us of the Temple sacrifice.

Betzah, a roasted egg, is a symbol of the ancient festival offering as well as a reminder of spring and rebirth.

Maror, a bitter herb, traditionally horseradish, recalls the bitter taste of slavery.

Karpas, a green vegetable such as parsley, is another symbol of spring.

Haroset reminds us of the brick mortar used by the Hebrew slaves. People of Eastern Europe make *haroset* from apples, nuts, and wine. Sephardic Jews use other recipes containing dates, raisins, and figs, the fruits of Mediterranean lands.

A separate plate of matzah, three pieces covered with a cloth, sits nearby.

Every place setting at the seder table gets a wine glass, even the children's (though many people fill the children's with grape juice). During the seder we drink four cups of wine.

A pillow is placed on the seder leader's chair or at all the places at the table. Participants in ancient Greek and Roman banquets reclined, while slaves stood throughout the meal. We recline in yet another joyous recognition of freedom.

We begin the seder with candle lighting and the Festival Kiddush over wine. Then the *karpas*, or green vegetable, is dipped in salt water, mixing the promise of spring green with the salt of slavery's tears.

Haggadah, matzah plate and cup for Elijah.

THE AFIKOMAN

The leader breaks the middle piece of matzah, setting one half aside for the *afikoman*. The *afikoman* is eaten at the end of the meal and no one can leave the Seder without tasting it.

A marvelous custom has grown up around the *afikoman*. The seder leader hides it, and the children try to find it. Since the adults cannot finish their meal without the *afikoman*, they must then negotiate a settlement, usually a gift, to ensure its return.

THE FOUR QUESTIONS

The Four Questions (*Mah Nishtanah*) bring us to the heart of the Haggadah. How is this night different from all other nights? Traditionally, the Four Questions are asked by the youngest child able to ask them, or by all the children present (see page 86 to help your child practice):

Why do we eat only matzah tonight?
Why do we eat bitter herbs on Pesah?
Why do we dip twice?
Why do we recline or lean back at the table?

Through these questions, the children are really asking for the reason we celebrate the Passover holiday. The Haggadah then gives us a set of answers.

ELIJAH'S CUP

After the meal, we fill a cup of wine for Elijah the Prophet and open the door for his arrival. Tradition says that Elijah will return one day to announce the coming of the Messiah. Perhaps this year will at last bring the long-awaited message of redemption.

PASSOVER FOR CHILDREN

In its most important aspects, Passover is for children. By explaining to them the rituals of Passover and by including them in our preparations—cleaning house, making *haroset*, searching for *hametz*, setting out the seder plate—we help them better understand the Passover seder itself and we prepare them to participate in it fully. In doing so, we endow them with the legacy of their heritage as Jews and fulfill God's commandment. "You shall tell your children on that day saying, 'It is because of what God did for me when I went free out of Egypt.' For God redeemed not only our ancestors, but us with them."

YOM HASHOAH

Let there be abundant peace from heaven...
From the Mourner's Kaddish

Yom Hashoah, literally "day of the calamity," commemorates the Holocaust. On this day, we remember the six million Jews who perished and, in doing so, confront head on questions about good and evil and God's role in the world.

IN THE SYNAGOGUE

Many newer prayerbooks contain rituals for Yom Hashoah. Many synagogues hold special prayer services. Sometimes whole communities come together to remember, to memorialize, and to recite the Mourner's Kaddish for those who were killed.

YOM HASHOAH FOR CHILDREN

As parents, we try to shield our children from pain and from evil. But as Jews we also have the obligation to remember all the individuals whose lives were lost. Part of this obligation must include a retelling of the tragedy to our children. We must speak to them of a man named Hitler who, like Haman, wanted to kill all the Jews. This time, however, there was no Queen Esther to save them, and six million Jews were murdered.

YOM HA'ATZMA'UT

The hope of two thousand years...
Hatikvah

Some Jews have always lived in the Land of Israel. In the late 1800's, others began returning to build new settlements there. This movement came partly in response to increasing anti-Semitism and escalating violence against Jews in Europe. However, the idea of reestablishing a Jewish state remained a radical and sometimes unpopular one for many years, even among Jews.

The publication of Theodore Herzl's tract *The Jewish State* in 1895 introduced the concept of political Zionism, and Herzl's efforts led to the convocation of a Jewish National Assembly and the establishment of the World Zionist Organization. Nevertheless, Herzl's dream of an internationally recognized, secure homeland for the Jewish people remained an elusive one for over half a century.

On the fifth of Iyar 5708, May 14, 1948, *Medinat Yisrael*, the State of Israel, was founded. The following day, Israel was attacked by five Arab armies but emerged victorious, a new nation with its own language—modern Hebrew.

With the rebirth of the State of Israel, Judaism exists both in its homeland and in the Diaspora. Yom Ha'atzma'ut, Independence Day, calls us to consider our relationship with Israel.

In Israel, Yom Ha'atzma'ut is preceded by Yom Ha-zikaron, the day of remembering those who died while fighting for the state. The solemnity of this day, which includes lighting candles and reciting prayers for the dead, is followed by the exuberance of celebration on Israel's Independence Day.

At the United Nations, the flag of the State of Israel flies among flags of other modern nations.

IN THE SYNAGOGUE

The establishment of Yom Ha'atzma'ut is so recent that the holiday lacks some of the ritualistic feel of other holidays. The Reform prayerbook includes a service written especially for this day, and the Conservative prayerbook contains a special prayer for the day.

YOM HA'ATZMA'UT FOR CHILDREN

For some children, connection with Israel takes the form only of an Israel bond purchased for them by Grandma and Grandpa when they were born. On Yom Ha'atzma'ut, however, we can strengthen their attachment to Israel—and our own—by celebrating the founding of the Jewish state. In large cities, the day is often marked by special parades. In many towns, the Jewish community center and synagogues celebrate the day with Israeli music, films, dancing, and food. As part of the festivities, it is a wonderful time to learn the Israeli National Anthem, *Hatikvah* (see page 87). Making paper flags to wave during the singing adds to the fun. And what better time to open a special bank account to begin saving for a trip to Israel with our children!

SHAVUOT

Every year in late spring, Jews celebrate the giving of the Torah with the festival of Shavuot.

When the people of Israel were gathered at the foot of Mount Sinai, God said to them, "What will you give Me as a surety pledge for the Torah?"

The Israelites answered, "We will pledge all our gold and silver as surety for the Torah."

But God did not accept this offer. "Even all the wealth in the world cannot measure up to this precious gift."

The Israelites tried again: "We will pledge our ancestors as surety."

"Your ancestors are in debt to Me," God replied. "How can they act as surety?"

The Israelites thought for a long time. Finally they offered to God their most precious possessions.

"We will pledge our children as surety for the Torah."

"I accept your children as surety," God said. "For their sake you will observe the Law."

—From a Midrash based on the Bible,
written about 1500 years ago

[55]

In biblical and Second Temple times, during the season of the Passover festival, farmers brought bundles of their first barley crop to Jerusalem. Waving these bundles, called *Omer*, before the altar, they thanked God for a good start to the growing season. From the beginning of Passover, farmers counted forty-nine days more until the "festival of first fruits," when they made another pilgrimage to Jerusalem, this time carrying bread loaves made from the summer's first wheat crop. The passing of forty-nine days, or seven weeks, lent the second festival its more familiar name, Shavuot, meaning "weeks." Shavuot always comes on the fiftieth day after Passover's beginning.

In this original form, as a nature festival and pilgrimage, Shavuot could have lost much of its relevance when the Jews lost their Temple and their agricultural life on the land. But the Rabbis gave new meaning to Shavuot. After a thorough study of the Book of Exodus, they determined that the Israelites came to Mount Sinai seven weeks after they left Egypt. Therefore, they agreed, Shavuot's real function was the anniversary of the giving of the Torah. This inspired conclusion elevated Shavuot beyond its agricultural base. Now, every year in late spring, Jews celebrate the giving of the Torah with the festival of Shavuot.

Omer Calendar.
40.1 France Mid-19th century. Attributed to Maurice Mayer, wood, glass, silver, cast engraved, partly gilt, semi-precious stones. From the collection of the Hebrew Union College Skirball Museum, Erich Hockley Photographer.

At Sinai, God and the people of Israel entered into a Covenant for all time. The Jews promised to observe God's Torah, for themselves, their children, and every succeeding generation. Shavuot reminds us of that everlasting Covenant and calls on us to look toward the future. We pledge ourselves not only to the distant memory of that epochal event at Sinai, but also to its faithful continuation.

Shavuot helps us to see ourselves as part of a long ladder reaching upward to Mount Sinai and to heaven.

[57]

Legend has it that Moses climbed such a ladder to receive the Torah, which he then carried down to the people below. The Torah has since traveled, rung by rung, down the ladder of generations. And now it is our turn to take the heritage of our parents and grandparents and, lovingly, pass it on to our children.

Shavuot still speaks to us of nature. The world is never more luscious than at this time of year, somewhere between spring and summer, when the sights and smells of green, growing things fill the senses. Traditionally, Jews welcome Shavuot by decorating the synagogue with plants and flowers, making the indoor environment as pleasant as the outdoors.

AT HOME

Shavuot opens with the candle blessing including the Sheheheyanu, Kiddush, and Ha-Motzi (see pages 72, 76, 77). Then the festival meal is eaten.

A sixteenth-century rabbi, Moses Isserles, wrote, "It is a universal custom to eat dairy foods on the first day of Shavuot." Although we know that the eating of sweet foods made from milk is a very old Shavuot custom, we have no clear idea how it got started. A legend states that the people got so hungry while waiting for Moses to come down from the mountain that they fixed a quick meal from fresh milk. A Hasidic rabbi declared, "When the

Jews received the Torah, they were considered as newborn infants who are only able to drink milk."

Yet another traditional explanation was that when the Israelites received the Torah, they realized that their cooking pots were not kosher and so ate a meal of cold dairy foods instead. Another plausible explanation lies in the biblical phrase "milk and honey," originally referring to the Land of Israel but later to Torah as well. We might say that the Torah tastes to us as delectable as a cheese blintz (see recipe page 95).

IN THE SYNAGOGUE

Throughout the generations, Jews have observed Shavuot with intense prayer and study. The sixteenth-century mystics spent the eve of Shavuot in the synagogue. All night long they studied the holy books, refreshing themselves with little cakes and an occasional sip of tea. They emerged at dawn and, squinting sleepy eyes at the sun, began a triumphant outdoor celebration of the festival service.

In our time, Jews continue to view this holiday as an affirmation of Jewish study and education. On Shavuot many congregations hold Confirmation ceremonies when religious school students of high school age declare their readiness to join the adult Jewish community. Conservative synagogues often celebrate graduation exercises from religious school on Shavuot.

The scriptural reading for the Shavuot service includes a portion from the Book of Ruth. This book portrays a peaceful, agricultural society—Israel in the time of the Judges. It contains one of the Bible's most moving passages.

Ruth declares her love for her mother-in-law, Naomi, and promises to stay always by her side:

> *Entreat me not to leave thee and to return from*
> *   following after thee;*
> *for wither thou goest, I will go; and where thou*
> *   lodgest, I will lodge;*
> *thy people will be my people, and thy God my God.*
>
> (Ruth 1:16)

SHAVUOT FOR CHILDREN

In some parts of Eastern Europe, Shavuot was the time when children were introduced to Torah study. Parents would prepare a slate with the Hebrew letters of the *alef-bet* and cover it with honey. Following the first hesitant steps to learn Hebrew, the child would lick the slate; later the adults would offer cake. And so, it was said, Jewish children came to know the sweetness of Torah.

The Ten Commandments, or "The Ten Words," as they are actually called in Hebrew, constitute the core of the revelation at Sinai. From their first proclamation to a small group of fugitive ex-slaves in the wilderness, they have found their way into the laws of two other religious civilizations and to universal acceptance throughout the modern world.

You can carry on the Shavuot tradition of education and Torah by teaching your children about the Ten Commandments. They are found in the Book of Exodus, beginning with chapter 20.

THE TEN COMMANDMENTS

1. I am your God, who brought you out of the land of Egypt. Do not worship any other gods but Me.
2. Do not worship idols.
3. Do not take the name of your God in vain.
4. Remember the Sabbath day and keep it holy.
5. Honor your father and mother.
6. Do not murder.
7. Do not commit adultery.
8. Do not steal.
9. Do not bear false witness against your neighbor.
10. Do not covet.

SHABBAT

And God blessed the seventh day...
Genesis 2:3

We all work and we all need rest. Often, in building a better life for ourselves and our children, we leave little time unstructured—time just to be ourselves, time to be with family, time to appreciate our Jewishness. Even our moments of physical rest can fail to refresh us, because we do not put aside the pressures and anxieties of the everyday world.

Judaism urges us to set one day apart. On the seventh day, Shabbat, we concentrate on things that are different. From sundown on Friday night to Saturday evening, we can appreciate the things that we are often too busy to notice during the week. We go to the synagogue, where we commemorate the work of our Creator and strengthen our ties with our Jewish community. We observe ceremonies that mark the uniqueness of the day. On Shabbat we enjoy family life, the foundation of all Jewish observance.

The original concept of Shabbat—a sanctified day of rest—is simple yet revolutionary, and writer after writer have added words of interpretation and acclaim. Shabbat is the only holiday to be included in the Ten Commandments. To our Rabbis, Shabbat represented the special relationship between God and the Jewish people. Medieval mystics described it as a union between the Shabbat "bride" and her happy groom, the people of Israel. And a masterpiece of Jewish mystical literature, the *Zohar*, likened Shabbat to a taste of redemption, calling it "a mirror of the world to come."

While Jews throughout the ages have praised Shabbat as the most important holiday that kept the people together, many non-Jewish commentators have seen Shabbat as Judaism's most important gift to the rest of the world. Until the introduction of a day of rest, the great majority of humanity toiled from dawn to dusk, day after day and week after week. The renowned psychologist Erich Fromm hailed Shabbat as a one-day release from "the chains of time."

No single source can do justice to the meaning and importance of the Jewish Sabbath. We hope these fragments will encourage you to seek more information. For Shabbat finds its most rewarding expression in the simple rituals followed at home. When you bring the fragrance of Shabbat into your family life, you bring yourself and your children closer to the very essence of Judaism.

AT HOME

Friday evening dinner is the quintessential Shabbat experience. Many families share this time with grandparents or close friends. As the stillness of Sabbath peace, "Shabbat Shalom," descends, we light at least two candles (see page 71). Tradition ascribes each light to a different biblical reference: the Book of Exodus commands, "remember the Sabbath day" (20:8), while Deuteronomy says, "observe the Sabbath day" (5:12). Some people light a candle for each member of the family.

Then comes a very special moment—the blessing of the children (see page 74). Through the gentle touch of your hands and the sound of your voice, your children will feel your love for them and your hopes for their future. This blessing is followed by the Shabbat Kiddush and the blessing over the bread (see pages 75 and 77).

On Shabbat we eat a special bread called hallah. The Hebrew word *hallah* first appears in the Torah, where it means a portion of bread set aside for the priests. Unlike the dark bread eaten throughout the week, it was made from white flour and probably tasted sweet, like cake. Later the word came to mean the special braided bread Jews throughout the world eat on Shabbat.

Hallah also calls to mind manna, the food that God supplied to the Israelites during their forty years' wandering in the wilderness of Sinai. The Bible relates that on Friday the people were instructed to gather two portions of manna, one for that day and one for Shabbat. Jews still remember this double manna portion by placing two hallah loaves on the Shabbat table. The loaves are covered with a decorated cloth, reminiscent of the dew sent by God to keep the manna fresh overnight.

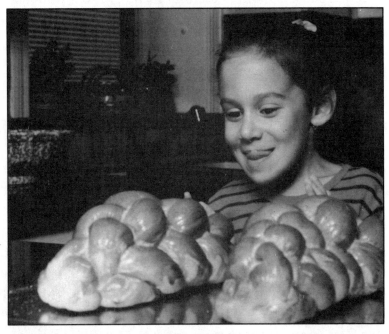

Baking hallah can be a shared family experience (see recipe page 96).

IN THE SYNAGOGUE

The mystics of the sixteenth-century Galilean community Ts'fat perceived Shabbat as a bride or queen. Every Friday evening, toward sunset, they gathered in the terraced fields outside the city and sang a welcoming greeting to their guest: "Come in peace...come in joy... come O bride, come!" Jews throughout the world still welcome the Sabbath with these words, which form part of the L'chah Dodi hymn sung at the beginning of the Friday evening service.

Since the time of the Bible, Judaism has established an increasingly elaborate set of restrictions and customs around Shabbat activity. All these rules have the same purpose—to emphasize the holiness of Shabbat by setting it apart from the other days of the week. The Jewish people have observed these laws and customs to enhance our enjoyment of Shabbat.

Attending synagogue services on Friday night or Saturday morning emphasizes the Shabbat difference. Here, through prayers, songs, and the reading of the weekly Torah portion, we celebrate the specialness of the Sabbath. Remembering that Shabbat is the day of rest, we seek relaxing pursuits for the remainder of the day that the whole family can share. Saturday afternoon is traditionally a time for a leisurely walk, visits with friends, and study.

HAVDALAH

So that the sweetness of Shabbat would last as long as possible, the Rabbis postponed its end until about an hour after sunset on Saturday. Before the era of clocks and watches, the stars were used to determine the end of Shabbat. When three stars are visible in the evening sky, it is time to bid farewell to Shabbat with the *Havdalah* ("separation") ceremony (see pages 78-79).

A braided candle and a box filled with aromatic spices such as cloves or cinnamon are used during the ceremony. The traditional song *Eliyahu Hanavi* is sung at the conclusion. The Prophet Elijah is known throughout the Jewish world as the herald of redemption. We may not know when redemption will come, but we can accurately predict the arrival of the next best thing—Shabbat, a mere six days away.

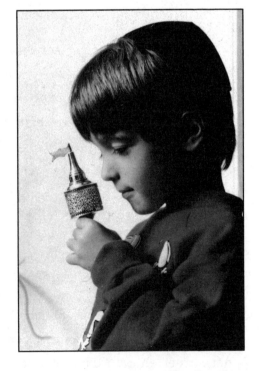

HOME RITUALS
FOR THE
HOLIDAYS

A Quick Guide to Home Celebration

On the following pages you will find blessings and prayers (in English and Hebrew along with a transliteration) for home observance of the Jewish holidays.

When you recite the blessings, try to follow the Hebrew form as it has been handed down for generations. If you cannot read the Hebrew, you can use the transliteration provided underneath each Hebrew text. Your children will find comfort in repeating the same structure again and again, holiday after holiday, year after year. They will hear mystery in the words and beauty in the old melodies. The blessings will become familiar, and soon your children will know the ceremonies by heart, without having consciously tried to memorize them. When you read prayers and blessings in English, you help your children to understand the meanings of the blessings you say together.

Feel free to pick and choose the parts of the various holiday services you wish to use, the ones you feel most comfortable with, the ones you and your children like the most. You may wish to begin by trying one ritual, such as lighting candles on Shabbat, and then add others over time. In this way your celebration of the holidays can grow as your children grow, and you truly make the traditions your own.

Candle Lighting

Light the candles. Move your hands around the flames several times and bring them toward your face. Place your hands in front of your face and recite the blessing:

בָּרוּךְ אַתָּה יְיָ אֱלֹהֵינוּ מֶלֶךְ הָעוֹלָם

אֲשֶׁר קִדְּשָׁנוּ בְּמִצְוֹתָיו וְצִוָּנוּ

לְהַדְלִיק נֵר שֶׁל שַׁבָּת.

Baruch atah adonai elohenu melech ha-olam asher kidshanu b'mitzvotav v'tzivanu l'hadleek ner shel shabbat.

Blessed are you, Adonai our God, Ruler of the world, who makes us holy with mitzvot, and commands us to kindle the Sabbath lights.

Continue with Blessing Your Children, page 74.

FOR FESTIVALS (except on Yom Kippur eve)
Candle Lighting

(When the Festival occurs on Shabbat, add the words in brackets.)

בָּרוּךְ אַתָּה יְיָ אֱלֹהֵינוּ מֶלֶךְ הָעוֹלָם
אֲשֶׁר קִדְּשָׁנוּ בְּמִצְוֹתָיו וְצִוָּנוּ
לְהַדְלִיק נֵר שֶׁל (שַׁבָּת וְ) יוֹם טוֹב.

Baruch atah adonai elohenu melech ha-olam asher kidshanu
b'mitzvotav v'tzivanu l'hadleek ner shel [shabbat v'] yom
tov.

Blessed are you, Adonai our God, Ruler of the world, who
makes us holy with mitzvot, and commands us to kindle the
[Sabbath and the] Festival lights.

בָּרוּךְ אַתָּה יְיָ אֱלֹהֵינוּ מֶלֶךְ הָעוֹלָם
שֶׁהֶחֱיָנוּ וְקִיְּמָנוּ וְהִגִּיעָנוּ לַזְּמַן הַזֶּה.

Baruch atah adonai elohenu melech ha-olam sheheheyanu
v'kiyemanu v'higiyanu la-zman ha-zeh.

Blessed are You, Adonai our God, Ruler of the world, who
has given us life, sustained us, and brought us to this
season of joy.

Continue with Festival Kiddush, page 76.

Candle Lighting

(When Yom Kippur occurs on Shabbat, add the words in brackets.)

בָּרוּךְ אַתָּה יְיָ אֱלֹהֵינוּ מֶלֶךְ הָעוֹלָם
אֲשֶׁר קִדְּשָׁנוּ בְּמִצְוֹתָיו וְצִוָּנוּ
לְהַדְלִיק נֵר שֶׁל (שַׁבָּת וְ) יוֹם הַכִּפּוּרִים.

*Baruch atah adonai elohenu melech ha-olam asher kidshanu
b'mitzvotav v'tzivanu l'hadleek ner shel [shabbat v'] yom
ha-kippurim.*

Blessed are You, Adonai our God, Ruler of the world, who
makes us holy with mitzvot, and commands us to kindle the
[Sabbath and the] Yom Kippur lights.

בָּרוּךְ אַתָּה יְיָ אֱלֹהֵינוּ מֶלֶךְ הָעוֹלָם
שֶׁהֶחֱיָנוּ וְקִיְּמָנוּ וְהִגִּיעָנוּ לַזְּמַן הַזֶּה.

*Baruch atah adonai elohenu melech ha-olam sheheḥeyanu
v'kiyemanu v'higiyanu la-zman ha-zeh.*

Blessed are You, Adonai our God, Ruler of the world, who
has given us life, sustained us, and brought us to this
season.

Blessing Your Children

(Place your hands on your child's head.)

For a daughter say:

יְשִׂימֵךְ אֱלֹהִים כְּשָׂרָה רִבְקָה רָחֵל וְלֵאָה.

Y'simech elohim k'sarah rivka raḥel v'leah.

May God make you like Sarah, Rebecca, Rachel, and Leah.

For a son say:

יְשִׂמְךָ אֱלֹהִים כְּאֶפְרַיִם וְכִמְנַשֶּׁה.

Y'simcha elohim k'efrayim v'chimenashe.

May God make you like Ephraim and Menasseh.

The blessing continues for all children:

יְבָרֶכְךָ יְיָ וְיִשְׁמְרֶךָ.

יָאֵר יְיָ פָּנָיו אֵלֶיךָ וִיחֻנֶּךָּ.

יִשָּׂא יְיָ פָּנָיו אֵלֶיךָ וְיָשֵׂם לְךָ שָׁלוֹם.

Y'varech'cha adonai v'yishm'recha. Ya'er adonai panav elecha viḥuneka. Yisa adonai panav elecha, v'yasem l'cha shalom.

May God bless you and keep you. May God's light shine on you and be gracious to you. May God's face be lifted upon you and give you peace.

Continue with Shabbat Kiddush, page 75.

FOR SHABBAT
Kiddush (Blessing Over the Wine)

(Hold the wine cup in your right hand as you recite the blessings:)

בָּרוּךְ אַתָּה יְיָ אֱלֹהֵינוּ מֶלֶךְ הָעוֹלָם
בּוֹרֵא פְּרִי הַגָּפֶן.

Baruch atah adonai elohenu melech ha-olam borei p'ree ha-gafen.

Blessed are you, Adonai, Ruler of the world, who creates the fruit of the vine.

For those who read Hebrew fluently:

בָּרוּךְ אַתָּה יְיָ אֱלֹהֵינוּ מֶלֶךְ הָעוֹלָם אֲשֶׁר קִדְּשָׁנוּ בְּמִצְוֹתָיו וְרָצָה בָנוּ
וְשַׁבַּת קָדְשׁוֹ בְּאַהֲבָה וּבְרָצוֹן הִנְחִילָנוּ, זִכָּרוֹן לְמַעֲשֵׂה בְרֵאשִׁית. כִּי הוּא
יוֹם תְּחִלָּה לְמִקְרָאֵי קֹדֶשׁ, זֵכֶר לִיצִיאַת מִצְרָיִם. כִּי-בָנוּ בָחַרְתָּ וְאוֹתָנוּ
קִדַּשְׁתָּ מִכָּל-הָעַמִּים, וְשַׁבַּת קָדְשְׁךָ בְּאַהֲבָה וּבְרָצוֹן הִנְחַלְתָּנוּ.

Blessed are You, Adonai, Ruler of the world, who makes us holy with mitzvot and shows us favor. You have made us holy by giving us Your commandments and have shown us Your favor. With love You have given us Your holy Sabbath which recalls the work of Creation. This day is the first of the holy festivals recalling our going forth from Egypt. You have chosen us from all peoples and made us holy and you have shown us Your loving favor by giving us Your holy Sabbath as a heritage.

בָּרוּךְ אַתָּה יְיָ מְקַדֵּשׁ הַשַּׁבָּת.

Baruch atah adonai m'kadesh ha-shabbat.

Blessed are you, Adonai, who sanctifies the Sabbath.

(Drink the wine.)

Complete the Shabbat Home Service with Ha-Motzi, page 77.

[75]

FOR FESTIVALS
Kiddush (Blessing over the Wine)

(Hold the wine cup in your right hand as you recite the blessings.)

בָּרוּךְ אַתָּה יְיָ אֱלֹהֵינוּ מֶלֶךְ הָעוֹלָם
בּוֹרֵא פְּרִי הַגָּפֶן.

Baruch atah adonai elohenu melech ha-olam borei p'ree ha-gafen.

Blessed are You, Adonai our God, Ruler of the world, creator of the fruit of the vine.

בָּרוּךְ אַתָּה יְיָ אֱלֹהֵינוּ מֶלֶךְ הָעוֹלָם
שֶׁהֶחֱיָנוּ וְקִיְּמָנוּ וְהִגִּיעָנוּ לַזְּמַן הַזֶּה.

Baruch atah adonai elohenu melech ha-olam sheheheyanu v'kiyemanu v'higiyanu la-zman ha-zeh.

Blessed are You, Adonai our God, Ruler of the world, who has given us life, sustained us, and brought us to this season of joy.

(Drink the wine.)

Complete the Festival Home Service with Ha-Motzi, page 77.

Ha-Motzi (Blessing over the Bread)

בָּרוּךְ אַתָּה יְיָ אֱלֹהֵינוּ מֶלֶךְ הָעוֹלָם

הַמּוֹצִיא לֶחֶם מִן הָאָרֶץ.

Baruch atah adonai elohenu melech ha-olam ha-motzi leḥem
min ha-aretz.

Blessed are You, Adonai our God, Ruler of the world, who
brings forth bread from the earth.

(Eat the bread.)

FOR THE CLOSE OF SHABBAT
HAVDALAH

Kiddush (Blessing Over the Wine)
(Fill the wine cup to overflowing, allowing some of the wine to spill onto the plate. Lift the cup.)

בָּרוּךְ אַתָּה יְיָ אֱלֹהֵינוּ מֶלֶךְ הָעוֹלָם
בּוֹרֵא פְּרִי הַגֶּפֶן.

Baruch atah adonai elohenu melech ha-olam borei p'ree ha-gafen.

Blessed are You, Adonai, Ruler of the world, who creates the fruit of the vine.

(Set the cup down.)

Blessing Over the Aromatic Spices
(Lift the spice holder.)

בָּרוּךְ אַתָּה יְיָ אֱלֹהֵינוּ מֶלֶךְ הָעוֹלָם
בּוֹרֵא מִינֵי בְשָׂמִים.

Baruch atah adonai elohenu melech ha-olam borei minay v'samim.

Blessed are You, Adonai, Ruler of the world, who creates all kinds of spices.

(Sniff the spices, then pass the spice box around to each person.)

[78]

Blessing Over the Havdalah Candle

בָּרוּךְ אַתָּה יְיָ אֱלֹהֵינוּ מֶלֶךְ הָעוֹלָם
בּוֹרֵא מְאוֹרֵי הָאֵשׁ.

Baruch atah adonai elohenu melech ha-olam

borei m'oray ha-esh.

Blessed are You, Adonai, Ruler of the world,

who creates the lights.

(Light the candle and hold it in your right hand.)

The final prayer speaks of *havdalah*, separation. The
twilight hour has passed. We have crossed the line
dividing Shabbat from the rest of the week.

בָּרוּךְ אַתָּה יְיָ אֱלֹהֵינוּ מֶלֶךְ הָעוֹלָם, הַמַּבְדִּיל בֵּין-קֹדֶשׁ
לְחֹל, בֵּין-אוֹר לְחֹשֶׁךְ, בֵּין -יִשְׂרָאֵל לָעַמִּים, בֵּין-יוֹם
הַשְּׁבִיעִי לְשֵׁשֶׁת יְמֵי-הַמַּעֲשֶׂה.

Praised are You, Adonai, Ruler of the world, who makes a
distinction between the sacred and secular, light and darkness, Israel and other peoples, the seventh day and the six
days of labor.

בָּרוּךְ אַתָּה יְיָ הַמַּבְדִּיל בֵּין-קֹדֶשׁ לְחֹל.

Baruch atah adonai ha-mavdeel bein kodesh l'ḥol.

Praised are You, Adonai, who makes a distinction between

sacred and secular.

(Everyone who wants takes a sip from the cup.
Then extinguish the candle in the wine on the plate.)

Blessings for the Sukkah

בָּרוּךְ אַתָּה יְיָ אֱלֹהֵינוּ מֶלֶךְ הָעוֹלָם
אֲשֶׁר קִדְּשָׁנוּ בְּמִצְוֹתָיו וְצִוָּנוּ לֵישֵׁב בַּסֻּכָּה.

Baruch atah adonai elohenu melech ha-olam asher kidshanu
b'mitzvotav v'tzivanu leishev ba-sukkah.

Blessed are You, Adonai our God, Ruler of the world, who makes us holy with mitzvot, and commands us to sit in the sukkah.

Blessing over the Lulav and Etrog

The blessing can be recited at home in the sukkah. Traditional Jews perform this ritual each day during Sukkot, except on Shabbat.

(Hold the etrog in your left hand, the lulav in your right.)

בָּרוּךְ אַתָּה יְיָ אֱלֹהֵינוּ מֶלֶךְ הָעוֹלָם
אֲשֶׁר קִדְּשָׁנוּ בְּמִצְוֹתָיו וְצִוָּנוּ עַל־נְטִילַת לוּלָב.

Baruch atah adonai elohenu melech ha-olam asher kidshanu
b'mitzvotav v'tzivanu al n'teelat lulav.

Blessed are you, Adonai our God, who has made us holy by giving us your commandments concerning the waving of the palm branch.

FOR ḤANUKKAH
Candle Lighting

As you face the Ḥanukkah menorah, place the first candle on your right. Subsequent candles are added to the left of it.

Light the *shamash*, take it in your hand, and say:

בָּרוּךְ אַתָּה יְיָ אֱלֹהֵינוּ מֶלֶךְ הָעוֹלָם
אֲשֶׁר קִדְּשָׁנוּ בְּמִצְוֹתָיו וְצִוָּנוּ
לְהַדְלִיק נֵר שֶׁל חֲנֻכָּה.

Baruch atah adonai elohenu melech ha-olam asher kidshanu b'mitzvotav v'tzivanu l'hadleek ner shel ḥanukkah.

Blessed are You, Adonai our God, Ruler of the world, who makes us holy with mitzvot, and commands us to kindle the Ḥanukkah lights.

בָּרוּךְ אַתָּה יְיָ אֱלֹהֵינוּ מֶלֶךְ הָעוֹלָם
שֶׁעָשָׂה נִסִּים לַאֲבוֹתֵינוּ
בַּיָּמִים הָהֵם בַּזְּמַן הַזֶּה.

Baruch atah adonai elohenu melech ha-olam she-asah nisim la-avoteinu ba-yameem ha-hem ba-zman ha-zeh.

Blessed are You, Adonai our God, Ruler of the world, who did wondrous things for our people long ago at this time of year.

Continue on next page.

On the first night of Ḥanukkah, we also recite the
Sheheḥeyanu blessing:

בָּרוּךְ אַתָּה יְיָ אֱלֹהֵינוּ מֶלֶךְ הָעוֹלָם
שֶׁהֶחֱיָנוּ וְקִיְּמָנוּ וְהִגִּיעָנוּ לַזְּמַן הַזֶּה.

Baruch atah adonai elohenu melech ha-olam shehecheyanu
v'kiyemanu v'higiyanu la-zman ha-zeh.

Blessed are You, Adonai our God, Ruler of the world, who
has given us life, sustained us, and brought us to this
season of joy.

(As you face the *hanukkiah*, light the candles with the *shamash*
from left to right. The newest candle is always lit first.)

FOR ḤANUKKAH
Maoz Tzur (Rock of Ages)

This song is traditionally sung right after the Ḥanukkah candles are lit.

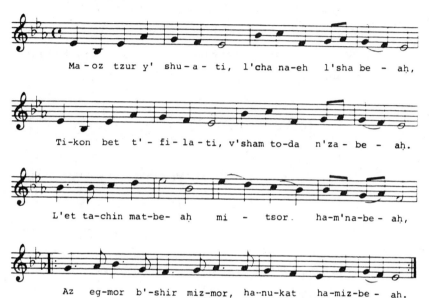

Ma - oz tzur y' shu-a - ti, l'cha na-eh l'sha be - ah,

Ti-kon bet t' - fi - la - ti, v'sham to-da n'za - be - ah.

L'et ta-chin mat-be- ah mi - tsor. ha-m'na-be - ah,

Az eg-mor b'-shir miz-mor, ha--nu-kat ha-miz-be - ah.

מָעוֹז צוּר יְשׁוּעָתִי, לְךָ נָאֶה לְשַׁבֵּחַ,
תִּכּוֹן בֵּית תְּפִלָּתִי, וְשָׁם תּוֹדָה נְזַבֵּחַ.

לְעֵת תָּכִין מַטְבֵּחַ, מִצָּר הַמְנַבֵּחַ,
אָז אֶגְמֹר בְּשִׁיר מִזְמוֹר, חֲנֻכַּת הַמִּזְבֵּחַ.

Rock of Ages, let our song praise Thy saving power;
Thou, amidst the raging foes, was our shelt'ring tower.
Furious, they assailed us, but Thine arm availed us,
And Thy word broke their sword, when our own strength failed us.

[83]

FOR PASSOVER
The Search for Leaven (Bedikat Ḥametz)

The Search for Leaven takes place on the night before the
first Passover seder. When the first evening of Passover
falls on Saturday night, this ritual is conducted on
Thursday. With the house dark, light the candle and say
this blessing:

בָּרוּךְ אַתָּה יְיָ אֱלֹהֵינוּ מֶלֶךְ הָעוֹלָם

אֲשֶׁר קִדְּשָׁנוּ בְּמִצְוֹתָיו וְצִוָּנוּ

עַל בִּעוּר חָמֵץ.

*Baruch atah adonai elohenu melech ha-olam asher kidshanu
b'mitzvotav v'tzivanu al biur ḥametz.*
Blessed are You, Adonai, Ruler of the world, who makes us
holy with mitzvot, and commands us to remove all the
leaven from our home.

The candle holder leads the way. Everyone else follows,
peering into the darkness for those stray crumbs of bread.
Use the feather to scoop the crumbs into the wooden spoon
or directly into the paper bag. When you have found all
the crumbs, put the feather and the spoon in the bag and
set it aside until morning.

The next morning:

Burn the bag and its contents. You can light a small fire in the backyard or in your driveway. While the ḥametz burns, formalize its removal with the following words:

Any leaven that may still be in this house, which I have not seen or have not removed, shall be as if it does not exist and as the dust of the earth.

From this moment the house is *pesaḥdik*--free of leaven. You are ready to celebrate the Passover holiday.

FOR PASSOVER
The Four Questions (Mah Nishtanah)

מַה נִּשְׁתַּנָּה הַלַּיְלָה הַזֶּה מִכָּל הַלֵּילוֹת?
שֶׁבְּכָל הַלֵּילוֹת אָנוּ אוֹכְלִין חָמֵץ וּמַצָּה
הַלַּיְלָה הַזֶּה כֻּלּוֹ מַצָּה.
שֶׁבְּכָל הַלֵּילוֹת אָנוּ אוֹכְלִין שְׁאָר יְרָקוֹת
הַלַּיְלָה הַזֶּה מָרוֹר.
שֶׁבְּכָל הַלֵּילוֹת אֵין אָנוּ מַטְבִּילִין
אֲפִילוּ פַּעַם אֶחָת
הַלַּיְלָה הַזֶּה שְׁתֵּי פְעָמִים.
שֶׁבְּכָל הַלֵּילוֹת אָנוּ אוֹכְלִין
בֵּין יוֹשְׁבִין וּבֵין מְסֻבִּין
הַלַּיְלָה הַזֶּה כֻּלָּנוּ מְסֻבִּין.

To help your child practice, here is a transliteration of the Four Questions:

Mah nishtanah halielah hazeh meekol haleilot?
Sheb'chol haleilot ahnu ochleen hametz u'matzah
halielah hazeh kuloh matzah.
Sheb'chol haleilot ahnu ochleen sh'ahr y'rahkot
halielah hazeh maror.
Sheb'chol haleilot ayn ahnu matbeeleen ahfeelu pa'ahm ehhat
halielah hazeh sh'tay f'ahmeem.
Sheb'chol haleilot ahnu ochleen bayn yosh'veen u'vayn m'subeen
halielah hazeh kulanu m'subeen.

FOR YOM HA'ATZMA'UT

Hatikvah (The Hope)

The National Anthem of the State of Israel

Kol__ ōd ba-lé-vav p'-ni-ma ne-fesh Y'-hu-di hō-mi-ya ul'-fa-a té miz-rach ka-di-ma a-yin l'-Tsi-yōn tsō-fi-ya ōd lō av-da tik-va-té-nu ha-tik-va bat shnōt al-pa-yim li-yōt am chof-shi b'-ar-tsé-nu e-rets Tsi-yōn Y'-ru-sha-la-yim li-yōt am chof-shi b'-ar-tsé-nu e-rets Tsi-yōn Y'-ru-sha-la-yim

As long as within the heart
a Jewish spirit is still alive
and the eyes look eastward toward Zion
our hope is not lost.
The hope of two thousand years
to be a free nation in our land
in the land of Zion and Jerusalem.

כָּל עוֹד בַּלֵּבָב פְּנִימָה
נֶפֶשׁ יְהוּדִי הוֹמִיָּה
וּלְפַאֲתֵי מִזְרָח קָדִימָה
עַיִן לְצִיּוֹן צוֹפִיָּה
עוֹד לֹא אָבְדָה תִקְוָתֵנוּ
הַתִּקְוָה בַּת שְׁנוֹת אַלְפַּיִם
לִהְיוֹת עַם חָפְשִׁי בְּאַרְצֵנוּ
אֶרֶץ צִיּוֹן וִירוּשָׁלָיִם

[87]

Secular Dates of Jewish Holidays

	1994	1995	1996	1997	1998	1999	2000	2001
Rosh Hashanah	Sept. 6	Sept. 25	Sept. 14	Oct. 2	Sept. 21	Sept. 11	Sept. 30	Sept. 18
Yom Kippur	Sept. 15	Oct. 4	Sept. 23	Oct. 11	Sept. 30	Sept. 20	Oct. 9	Sept. 27
Sukkot	Sept. 20	Oct. 9	Sept. 28	Oct. 16	Oct. 5	Sept. 25	Oct. 14	Oct. 2
Simhat Torah	Sept. 28	Oct. 17	Oct. 6	Oct. 24	Oct. 13	Oct. 3	Oct. 22	Oct. 10
Hanukkah	Nov. 28	Dec. 18	Dec. 6	Dec. 24	Dec. 14	Dec. 4	Dec. 22	Dec. 10

	1995	1996	1997	1998	1999	2000	2001	2002
Tu B'Shevat	Jan. 16	Feb. 5	Jan. 23	Feb. 11	Feb. 1	Jan. 22	Feb. 8	Jan. 28
Purim	Mar. 16	Mar. 5	Mar. 23	Mar. 12	Mar. 2	Mar. 21	Mar. 9	Feb. 26
Passover	Apr. 15	Apr. 4	Apr. 22	Apr. 11	Apr. 1	Apr. 20	Apr. 8	Mar. 28
Yom Hashoah	Apr. 27	Apr. 16	May 4	Apr. 23	Apr. 13	May 2	Apr. 20	Apr. 9
Yom Ha'azma'ut	May 5	Apr. 24	May 12	May 1	Apr. 21	May 10	Apr. 28	Apr. 17
Shavuot	June 4	May 24	June 11	May 31	May 21	Jun 9	May 28	May 17

HOLIDAY RECIPES

Each holiday has its own special flavor. Holiday foods do more than satisfy our taste buds—they keep alive that old-time festival atmosphere that has always been a part of the Jewish experience. In this respect, we are just like every generation before us. We cannot imagine a happy celebration without delicious holiday foods.

On the following pages you will find recipes for a few traditional favorites to get you started. They are easy to follow and they taste good. But, most important, they can be prepared by parents and children together.

FOR ROSH HASHANAH

Taiglach (Honey Candy)

Choose a bright, sunny day to make this honey candy.
Moisture in the air will keep it from hardening.

2 eggs	1 cup honey
2 tablespoons vegetable oil	1/2 cup sugar
1 1/2 cups flour	1/2 teaspoon ground ginger
1/2 teaspoon salt	1 cup nuts, coarsely broken
3/4 teaspoon baking powder	

Beat eggs slightly. Add the oil and mix.

Sift the flour, salt, and baking powder together. Stir into the egg and oil mixture to make a soft, but not sticky, dough. Add more flour if necessary.

Place the dough on a board, lightly sprinkle with flour, and twist it into a rope shape about 1/3 inch thick. Dip a knife in flour, and cut the rope of dough into small pieces about 1/3 inch long.

Place the pieces on a well greased shallow pan and bake in a moderately hot oven (375°) for about 10 minutes, or until slightly browned. Shake the pan a few times to keep the pieces separated and evenly browned.

Now prepare the honey syrup. Put the honey, sugar, and ginger in a saucepan. Stir until the sugar is completely melted. Now cook it gently over a low flame for 5 minutes, stirring constantly, for honey will burn quickly.

Add the baked pieces of dough and the nuts. Stir gently over low heat until the mixture is a deep golden brown.

Pour out on a large platter or board wet with cold water.

Shape the candy into a cake about 8 inches square and 2 inches deep using a knife wet with cold water. Cut into 2-inch strips and cut again into bite-sized pieces.

When cool, wrap in waxed paper.

Makes 36 to 48 pieces of candy.

Apple Strudel

For the dough	For the filling
2 1/2 cups flour	jam or marmalade
1/2 teaspoon baking powder	8 apples, pared and chopped
1/2 teaspoon salt	1 cup raisins, chopped
1/4 cup sugar	1 cup nuts, coarsely chopped
1 egg	sugar
1/2 cup oil	cinnamon
1/2 cup lukewarm water	

Sift flour, baking powder, salt, and sugar into a mixing bowl.
Make a well in the center of the mixture and into it drop the egg,
oil, and water. Beat these with a fork. Then stir in the flour
mixture to make a soft dough, one that is not sticky and is easy to
handle. Sprinkle a board lightly with flour. Divide the dough
into three parts. Roll one piece of dough until it is paper-thin.
Should it tear, mend it by pressing a piece of dough from the
edge to the torn part. Spread the dough with a thin layer of jam
or marmalade. Now sprinkle on 1/3 of the chopped apples,
raisins, nuts, sugar, and cinnamon.

Roll the dough lengthwise like a jelly roll. Press the edges
together to keep the filling in. Repeat these steps with the other
two pieces of dough.

Place the three rolls on a well-greased baking sheet. Leave space
between the rolls to allow them to bake evenly. Brush the top of
each roll with oil, and sprinkle them with sugar and cinnamon.
Bake in a moderately hot oven (375°) for 45 minutes, or until
golden brown. Remove from oven. When cool, cut into
1 1/2 inch slices.

Makes about 60 small pieces of strudel.

Latkes

4 large potatoes

2 eggs

1 teaspoon salt

3 tablespoons flour

1/2 teaspoon baking powder

oil for frying

Wash and peel potatoes. Grate by hand or use food processor.
Drain off most of the liquid.
Beat eggs and mix all ingredients together, except oil.
Drop mixture by tablespoons into hot oil in skillet.
Fry on both sides until brown.
Drain on paper towels.
Serve with applesauce or sour cream.
Serves 4.

Note: Do not fry more than three or four latkes at the same time.
Too many fried at once will cool the oil and keep the latkes from
being crisp and tender.

Hamantashen

1/2 cup butter or margarine

1 cup sugar

1 egg

1 tablespoon milk

1 teaspoon vanilla extract

2 cups flour

2 teaspoons baking powder

1/4 teaspoon salt

fruit preserves, prune jam (*lekvar*) or poppy seeds (*mohn*)

Cream the butter and gradually add sugar.
Beat the mixture until fluffy.
Add egg, milk, and vanilla and beat well.
Sift flour, baking powder, and salt together and add to mixture.
Stir to make a soft dough.
Chill in the refrigerator for 20 minutes.
Sprinkle a board lightly with flour. Roll the dough out on the
board until it is about 1/8 inch thick.
Dip a wide-mouthed jar or glass into flour and cut circles from
dough. Spoon some preserves or jam in the center of each circle.
Bring three sides of the circle together to form a triangle, leaving
about one-third open in the center. Pinch the edges together to
make a seam.
Arrange well apart on an ungreased baking sheet. Bake in a hot
oven (400°) for 10-12 minutes.

Makes about 36 hamantashen.

Matzah Balls

2 eggs

1/4 cup water

3 tablespoons melted shortening

1 teaspoon salt

dash of pepper

1/2 cup matzah meal

Beat the eggs lightly with a fork.
Add the water, melted shortening, salt, and pepper, and mix well.
Add the matzah meal and stir thoroughly.
Refrigerate for 1 hour.
Wet your hands and form mixture into small balls.
Drop balls into a large pot of boiling water or chicken soup.
Cover and simmer 20-25 minutes.
Serve in chicken soup.

Makes about 16 matzah balls.

FOR SHAVUOT

Cheese Blintzes

For the pancake
2 eggs
1/2 teaspoon salt
1 cup milk
1 cup flour, sifted
butter

For the filling
1 pound. dry cottage cheese or farmer cheese
1 egg
salt and pepper or sugar to taste

Beat 2 eggs with salt until light and fluffy.
Stir in milk and add to sifted flour to make a smooth, thin batter.
Melt a very small amount of butter in a 6-inch skillet.
Pour in just enough batter to cover bottom of pan (about 2 tablespoons) and tilt the pan from side to side. Cook gently for a minute or two until edges of blintz dry and pull away from pan.
Turn out with sharp tap onto a towel to cool.
Stack them after they cool.
Blend cottage cheese, egg, and salt and pepper or sugar in blender or with electric mixer until smooth.
Place a heaping tablespoon of filling on the fried side of each pancake. Fold three sides over the cheese filling. Then roll the pancake, tucking in the edges to keep the filling in.
Fry in butter or oil until golden brown, turning once. Or bake in 350° oven until crisp and brown.
Serve with sour cream or jam.

Makes 16 blintzes.

Ḥallah

This is a two-part recipe; the dough must be refrigerated overnight.

1 package dry yeast	3 eggs
1/4 cup plus 2 tablespoons sugar	1/3 cup oil
1 cup lukewarm water	1/2 cup warm water
5 cups flour	1 1/4 to 1 1/2 cups flour
1 tablespoon plus teaspoon salt	1 egg

On Thursday:
Add yeast and sugar to 1 cup of lukewarm water and stir until dissolved. Put 5 cups of flour into a large bowl and make a well in the middle. Add salt, 3 eggs, oil, and yeast mixture and mix thoroughly. Add 1/2 cup of warm water. Stir in additional 1 1/4 to 1 1/2 cups of flour to make a stiff yet easy-to-handle dough. Turn out on floured surface and knead for several minutes until smooth, sprinkling with flour if dough is sticky. Grease a large glass bowl and place the dough in the bowl, turning once so both sides are greased. Cover with a towel and let dough rise in a warm place (pre-heat oven, then turn off) for 1 hour. Dough will rise only slightly. Punch down the dough and cover it with plastic wrap and a towel, and refrigerate overnight.

On Friday:
Punch down the dough and make two loaves by dividing the dough into six pieces: Shape into strips and then braid, using three strips for each loaf. Pinch ends of strips together. Place on greased baking sheets. Cover and let rise for 30 to 40 minutes in a warm place. Brush loaves lightly with a beaten egg. Bake at 350° for 30 to 35 minutes until golden brown. To test for doneness, a thump on the bottom should give a hollow sound.